A BRIEF ILLUSTRATED
HISTORY of
SPACE
EXPLORATION

ROBERT SNEDDEN
&
DAVID WEST

CAPSTONE PRESS
a capstone imprint

First published in hardcover by Capstone Press, an imprint of Capstone, in 2017
1710 Roe Crest Drive, North Mankato, Minnesota 56003
www.mycapstone.com

Library of Congress Cataloging-in-Publication Data
Names: Snedden, Robert, author. | West, David, 1956- author.
Title: A brief illustrated history of space exploration / by Robert Snedden
and David West.
Other titles: Space exploration
Description: North Mankato, Minnesota : Capstone Press, [2017] | Series: Fact
finders. A brief illustrated history | Audience: Ages 8-11. | Audience:
Grades 4 to 6. | Includes bibliographical references and index.
Identifiers: LCCN 2016041881 |
ISBN 9781515725190 (library binding)
Subjects: LCSH: Manned space flight—History—Juvenile literature. | Space
probes—History—Juvenile literature. | Space flight—History—Juvenile
literature. | Outer space—Exploration—History—Juvenile literature.
Classification: LCC TL793 .S6195 2017 | DDC 629.4—dc23
LC record available at https://lccn.loc.gov/2016041881

A BRIEF ILLUSTRATED HISTORY OF SPACE EXPLORATION
was produced by
David West Children's Books, 6 Princeton Court, 55 Felsham Road, London SW15 1AZ

Copyright © 2017 David West Children's Books

Designed and illustrated by David West
Text by Robert Snedden
Editor Brenda Haugen

Printed in China
007966
Photographic credits: page 10, Alex Zelenko; page 12bl, Mike Peel, Jodrell Bank Centre for Astrophysics,
University of Manchester; page 22b, ESA

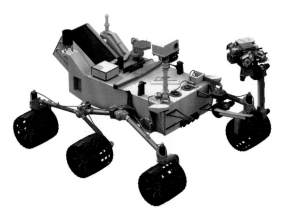

TABLE OF CONTENTS

INTRODUCTION
4

ROCKETEERS
EARLY IDEAS OF SPACE TRAVEL
TO THE FIRST ROCKETS
6

THE SPACE RACE
USSR VERSUS USA
8

THE SPACE RACE
THE FIRST PEOPLE IN SPACE
10

THE SPACE RACE
EARLY SATELLITES
12

THE SPACE RACE
EARLY SPACE PROBES
13

THE SPACE RACE
SPACEWALKERS
14

THE SPACE RACE
MAN ON THE MOON
15

END OF THE SPACE RACE
ERA OF THE SPACE STATIONS
16

SPACE SHUTTLE
THE SPACE TRANSPORTATION
SYSTEM
18

INTERNATIONAL SPACE STATION
(ISS)
20

EYES AND EARS IN SPACE
MODERN SATELLITES
22

MODERN SPACE PROBES
TO THE SUN, MOON, AND
INNER PLANETS
24

MODERN SPACE PROBES
TO THE OUTER PLANETS AND
BEYOND
26

SPACE EXPLORATION
THE FUTURE
28

GLOSSARY
30

INDEX
32

INTRODUCTION

Jules Verne's novel, From the Earth to the Moon, *published in 1865, fired the idea of space travel in people's imaginations.*

POSSIBLY FOR AS LONG AS THERE HAVE BEEN HUMANS, PEOPLE HAVE LOOKED AT THE NIGHT SKY AND WONDERED WHAT WAS UP THERE. It is only very recently in our history, 60 years or so, that we have had the means to go and take a look. The achievement of putting first satellites and then people into orbit around Earth was front page news around the world. The first astronauts were celebrated as heroes. Now people can go back and forth to the *International Space Station* with scarcely a mention.

At the beginning of the Space Age in the 1950s, only two countries, the United States and the Soviet Union (USSR), had the capability to launch spacecraft into orbit and beyond. Today there are 13 government agencies with launch capability, including the European Space Agency, China, India, and Japan. All have long-term objectives for exploring space. Although there are plans for people to return to the Moon and even to venture to Mars, for now all exploration is carried out by space probes such as *Juno*, *Rosetta*, and *Cassini*. These robot adventurers don't need food, water, or air and can travel to places no people could survive. They are sent out to the farthest parts of the Solar System. The results have been amazing. The information received from them is an ongoing inspiration, urging humankind to explore ever farther.

Rockets at war
Rockets were first used in war by the Chinese in 1232 against the Mongols. Over the next few centuries, the technology spread to other countries and continued to develop. In 1812 rockets designed by Sir William Congreve for the British army were used against the United States in the War of 1812. This was "the rockets' red glare" described in The Star Spangled Banner *(left).*

Animal rocketeer
Claude Ruggieri, an Italian living in Paris, successfully launched a number of animals into the air by rocket, including, in 1830, a ram that reached a height of 650 feet (200 meters) using a cluster of rockets. A parachute returned it to Earth unharmed. Ruggieri's plans for the first human rocket flight were stopped when the test passenger was found to be an 11-year-old boy (right).

ROCKETEERS
EARLY IDEAS OF SPACE TRAVEL TO THE FIRST ROCKETS

At the beginning of the 20th century, a number of scientists and engineers began exploring ideas of using rockets as a means to explore space and extend our knowledge. But there were also those who wanted to develop rockets further as devastating weapons of war.

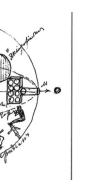

Konstantin Tsiolkovsky (left) designed spaceships (right) that would spin to provide gravity.

First ideas

Russian school teacher Konstantin Tsiolkovsky (1857–1935) had ideas for space exploration using liquid-fuelled rockets and space habitats in 1903. Although he never built a rocket, he has been described as the father of modern astronautics because of his ideas. American Robert Goddard (1882–1945) flew the world's first liquid-fuelled rocket in Massachusetts on March 16, 1926. The rocket flew less than 200 feet (60 m), but local fire marshals were so alarmed, they barred him from further experiments. Goddard moved to New Mexico and developed the first gyro-controlled rocket guidance system. In 1923 the book *The Rocket Into Interplanetary Space* was published by German space pioneer Hermann Oberth (1894–1989). Its ideas inspired rocket societies around the world.

Robert Goddard tows one of his rockets to its launch site in Roswell, New Mexico, in 1932.

German pyrotechnics engineer Wilhelm Friedrich Sander (left) provided rocket engines for Fritz von Opel (standing right).

Austrian Max Valie, another rocket pioneer, also worked with Opel. In 1930 he drove one of the first liquid fuel rocket cars (right).

Rocket cars

In the 1920s, the German Opel car company produced a number of rocket-powered cars. These cars were really built as publicity for the company and were never intended to go into production. The cars were powered by solid fuel rockets, ran on rails, and reached speeds of more than 125 miles (200 km) per hour. After one car exploded, the railway authorities stopped Opel's test runs. The rockets were built by Wilhelm Friedrich Sander, who was also involved in building the first rocket-powered glider with Opel. An exploding rocket set the glider alight on its second flight. The pilot landed before the glider was destroyed.

Sergei Korolev (seated center), was the founder of GIRD, the rocket society that developed the first Soviet liquid-fuelled rockets in the 1930s. Later, as the Soviet's lead rocket engineer, he was responsible for putting the first people in space.

Rocket societies

Russian engineer Sergei Korolev (1907–1966) designed his first glider when he was only 17. He grew interested in rocket propulsion and, in 1931, founded the Group for Investigation of Reactive Motion (GIRD), which developed the first Soviet liquid-fuelled rockets. The group also designed the RP-318, a Soviet rocket-powered piloted glider.

Another group of budding rocketeers, including Oberth, began working for the German army in 1932. The Germans, banned from having long-range artillery after World War I (1914–1918), were interested in using rockets as weapons. The group, led by Wernher von Braun, began to produce a series of liquid-fuelled rockets in 1937. This led to the V-2, the world's first long-range ballistic missile.

The V-2

Just 46 feet (14 m) long, the V-2 was smaller than many of today's rockets. Its engines burned liquid oxygen and alcohol to produce a huge thrust. It could carry 1,500 pounds (700 kilograms) of explosives over 200 miles (320 kilometers) at speeds approaching 2,500 miles (4,000 km) per hour. Between September 1944 and March 1945, more than 1,000 V-2 rockets were launched at London, England, causing great damage, but they could not

prevent Germany's defeat in World War II (1939–1945). The many German rocket engineers and V-2s captured by the United States and the Soviet Union formed the base for space exploration and missile development after the war.

More than 3,000 V-2 missiles were launched against Allied cities (left).

the internal structure of the V-2

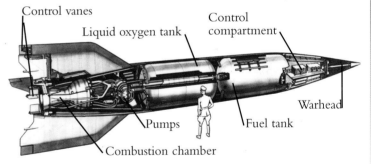

Control vanes
Liquid oxygen tank
Control compartment
Warhead
Pumps
Fuel tank
Combustion chamber

Rocket fighter planes

The Messerschmitt Me 163 Komet was the world's first, and only, rocket-powered fighter aircraft. Designed by German aeronautical engineer Alexander Lippisch, the Komet had no tailplane or landing gear, which saved weight. It took off from a detachable wheeled bogie and landed on a light skid, instead of wheels. A small propeller at the front of the craft generated electricity for the instruments. The fuel-hungry Komet had a speed of 600 miles (960 km) per hour but a range of only 50 miles (80 km).

The German rocket-powered Messerschmitt Me 163 fighter aircraft was flown during World War II.

THE SPACE RACE
USSR VERSUS USA

Following the end of World War II the United States and Soviet Union used captured German equipment and knowledge to develop the Intercontinental Ballistic Missile (ICBM). Intended as a weapon, the power of the ICBM's rocket motors would also make space flight possible.

German rocket engineers Walter Dornberger, Herbert Axter, Wernher von Braun, and Hans Lindenberg after their surrender to the Allies in 1945 (von Braun had been injured in a car accident)

The first images of Earth from space were taken by a V-2 rocket, launched from the United States on October 24, 1946.

Postwar United States

U.S. forces captured enough V-2 parts to assemble around 80 rockets. Wernher von Braun also fell into American hands. The V-2s were used as sounding rockets, launched to high altitudes to explore Earth's upper atmosphere but not entering orbit. The explosive

On October 14, 1947, Captain Charles "Chuck" Yeager became the first person to break the sound barrier in the Bell X-1, reaching Mach 1.06 (700 miles, 1,100 km, per hour). The rocket-powered plane was dropped from a bomber. It glided to Earth once out of fuel.

warhead of the V-2 was replaced by scientific instruments.

The development of ever more powerful rockets in the years after World War II was not simply a result of scientific curiosity. It became a race between the United States and the Soviet Union to produce a delivery system for a new weapon—the atomic bomb. The Soviet Union's hydrogen bomb weighed 2.2 tons (2 metric tons), a real challenge for the rocket engineers. Sergei Korolev designed the R7 rocket with small engines clustered around a central core. On its first successful flight in 1957, it travelled 4,000 miles (6,400 km).

Redstone to Kaputnik

The first large ballistic U.S. missile was the PGM-11 Redstone. It was developed from the V-2 by the German rocket engineers captured at the end of World War II. Designed to carry a nuclear warhead, it became one of the most reliable rockets of its day.

Having witnessed the Soviet's successful launch of *Sputnik 1*, the Americans were determined to catch up. A small experimental satellite was quickly added to a test flight of the new Vanguard rocket. On December 6, 1957, the U.S. Navy launched the rocket from Cape Canaveral. It exploded on liftoff. The satellite was blown into some bushes, where it started transmitting signals. The American press called the failure Kaputnik.

The PGM-11 Redstone was the first large American ballistic missile.

The first satellite to be launched by the United States exploded on the launch pad.

Multistage rockets

The R7 was a multistage rocket, a type made up of one or more rockets either stacked on top of one another or attached alongside each other. The R7 had four strap-on boosters attached to the second stage rocket. Multistage rockets were developed by Tsiolkovsky, Oberth, and Goddard. The first high-speed multistage rockets were the RTV G4 Bumper rockets, which combined a V–2 with a WAC Corporal sounding rocket. The greatest altitude they reached was 244 miles (393 km).

A two-stage Bumper 8 rocket, was the first launch from Cape Canaveral, Florida. In the years that followed the July 1950 launch, Cape Canaveral became the heart of the American space program.

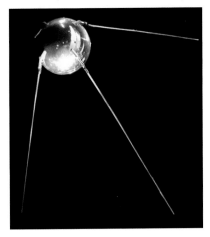

Sputnik 1, the first satellite, was a 23-inch- (58-centimeter-) diameter metal sphere, with radio antennae to broadcast radio pulses.

USSR and the first satellites

On October 4, 1957, people around the world woke to find that for the first time there was an artificial object in orbit around Earth. Launched by the USSR using an R7 rocket, *Sputnik 1*, the first satellite, seemed to take everyone by surprise. For many, it was hard to believe that people had sent an object hurtling around the planet at more than 18,000 miles (29,000 km) per hour. A month later the USSR launched a second satellite. *Sputnik 2* brought another surprise. Inside was a dog named Laika —the first living thing to reach orbit. But Laika did not survive the trip into space. Overheating and the stress of space travel caused her death a few hours into the flight.

Sputnik 2 was launched on November 3, 1957, and carried the first living animal, a dog named Laika, into space.

Explorer 1 *(above) was launched into orbit by a four-stage* Juno I *rocket (left) from Cape Canaveral, Florida, USA.*

U.S. success with *Explorer 1*

After the failure of *Vanguard*, the United States successfully launched its first satellite, *Explorer 1*, on January 31, 1958. One of *Explorer's* discoveries was that "belts" of radiation, the Van Allen Belts, surround Earth. The particles in these belts can damage instruments in satellites and are also a danger to any astronauts passing through them.

Later that year, on July 29, 1958, the National Aeronautics and Space Administration (NASA) was set up for the American space program.

THE SPACE RACE
THE FIRST PEOPLE IN SPACE

BOTH THE UNITED STATES AND THE USSR KNEW THAT THE FIRST COUNTRY TO PUT PEOPLE INTO ORBIT AND BRING THEM HOME SAFELY WOULD WIN GREAT STATUS IN THE WORLD. SOON AFTER THE FIRST SATELLITES WERE LAUNCHED, BOTH COUNTRIES WERE MAKING PLANS TO DO JUST THAT. THE SPACE RACE WAS ON.

Yuri Gagarin, 1961

The first cosmonauts

The United States selected its first astronauts in 1959 but lacked a booster powerful enough to carry them into space. The USSR was very much the frontrunner in the Space Race. The first human in space was cosmonaut Yuri Gagarin, who made a single orbit of Earth in *Vostok 1* on April 12, 1961. He was carried aloft by an improved version of Korolev's powerful R-7 rocket. His flight lasted for 108 minutes and reached a height of 203 miles (327 km) above Earth. He was the first person ever to see Earth from space.

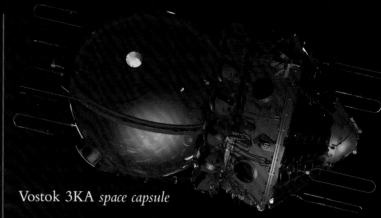

Vostok 3KA *space capsule*

Gagarin exited the capsule and parachuted back to Earth after the craft reentered Earth's atmosphere. Five more Vostok flights were made. In June 1963 Valentina Tereshkova, aboard *Vostok 6*, was the first woman to orbit Earth.

Valentina Tereshkova spent almost three days in space, orbiting Earth 48 times in 1963.

Dogs in space

Before sending the first cosmonaut into orbit, the USSR tested its launch vehicles using dogs. In July 1951 Dezik and Tsygan were the first dogs to make a suborbital flight, reaching an altitude of 68 miles (110 km) before returning safely to Earth. Many more dog flights were made, three reaching 280 miles (450 km) above Earth. Laika, the first dog into orbit, was followed by Belka and Strelka in August 1960, the first to orbit Earth and return alive. The longest dog spaceflight was 22 days—spent in orbit by Veterok and Ugolyok in February 1966.

A stamp (left) commemorates the flight of dogs Belka and Strelka and many other animals aboard Korabl-Sputnik 2 in 1960, the first space mission to send animals into orbit and return them safely to Earth.

The R-7 rockets (right) were the first with the power to transport objects into Earth's orbit.

Project Mercury

The first of America's manned space programs was Project Mercury. Lacking a booster rocket to match the Soviet's R-7, the Americans kept the Mercury space capsule small and simple. It weighed just 3,000 pounds (1,360 kg) and was about 6.5 feet (2 m) long. The Vostok spacecraft by comparison weighed 5.5 tons (5 metric tons). The seven astronauts selected for training were all military test pilots.

In May 1961 Alan Shepard became the first American to reach space, though the Redstone rocket used to launch his Mercury craft didn't have the power to send it into orbit. Shepard's mission lasted just 15 minutes.

The second Mercury mission was also suborbital. It nearly ended in disaster when astronaut Virgil "Gus" Grissom's capsule's hatch cover blew off after splashdown. Water flooded the spacecraft and Grissom's spacesuit started to fill. He was rescued but the capsule sank. It was finally recovered 38 years later.

At last, on February 20, 1962, John Glenn became the first American to orbit Earth, boosted into space by the more powerful Atlas D rocket. Three successful Mercury flights followed.

Alan Shepard, the first American in space

John Glenn was the first American to orbit Earth.

A Mercury-Redstone rocket launched Alan Shepherd into suborbital flight on May 5, 1961. After reentry the capsule parachuted into the Atlantic Ocean off the Bahamas. From there it was recovered by helicopter and taken to an aircraft carrier.

John Glenn's Mercury capsule orbits Earth.

Chimpanzee in space

On January 31, 1961, a chimpanzee named Ham was sent on a 16-minute suborbital flight in a Mercury-Redstone capsule. He was named after the Holloman Aerospace Medical Center where he was trained to carry out simple tasks. The purpose of the mission was to check the craft's environmental control and recovery systems and test how the life support system performed in zero gravity. Ham's safe return paved the way for Alan Shepard's flight a few months later.

After his flight, chimpanzee Ham is greeted by the commander of the recovery ship, USS Donner.

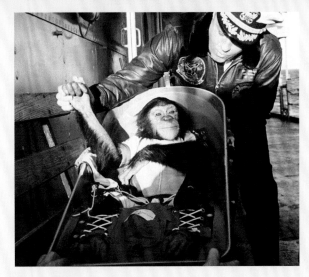

THE SPACE RACE
EARLY SATELLITES

AFTER THE SUCCESSFUL LAUNCHES OF SPUTNIK AND EXPLORER, SPACE BEGAN TO GET A LOT BUSIER. SOVIET AND AMERICAN SCIENTISTS AND ENGINEERS COMPETED WITH EACH OTHER TO GATHER MORE INFORMATION ABOUT CONDITIONS FAR ABOVE THE SURFACE OF EARTH. THE AGE OF THE SATELLITE HAD BEGUN.

Solar panel

Launched in 1958 Vanguard I *is the oldest satellite in orbit. It was the first to use solar power.*

After Sputnik

Within about three years after the launch of *Sputnik 1,* there were 100 or more satellites in orbit around Earth. In August 1959 *Explorer 6* sent back the first fuzzy black and white picture of Earth seen from orbit. Less than a year later, the *TIROS-1* weather satellite was sending back television pictures of the planet.

Communications satellites

The first communications satellite, *Echo 1*, launched on August 12, 1960. It was simply a giant metal balloon more than 100 feet (30 m) across, from which radio signals were bounced. *Echo 1* was nicknamed a "satelloon" by the project's NASA team.

The weather satellite TIROS-1 sent the first television image of Earth from space.

Telstar 1, *launched in 1962, relayed the first live transatlantic television pictures.*

Communications satellites soon became more sophisticated. *Telstar,* launched in 1962, was the first active communications satellite. Although it only operated for a few months from July 10, 1962, to February 21, 1963, *Telstar* captured the world's imagination. It was the beginning of the revolution of satellites relaying information to and from all parts of Earth that everyone takes for granted today.

Syncom 3 *was the first geostationary communications satellite. Launched in 1964 it telecast the 1964 Summer Olympic Games in Tokyo to the United States.*

The Lovell radio telescope at Jodrell Bank Observatory in Cheshire, England, was completed in 1957. It tracked space probes, such as Sputnik 1, at the start of the Space Age.

Ground stations

There is little point in satellites and space probes gathering information if we can't see it. This is where ground receiving stations come in. Designed to communicate with spacecraft, a ground station is a radio station. It uses large antennae to pick up the faint signals from satellites and from even more distant space probes.

Ground stations are so sensitive, they can pick up signals no more powerful than an ordinary light bulb, sent from a probe millions of miles away.

The first dish at Goonhilly Satellite Earth Station in Cornwall, England, Antenna One (dubbed Arthur), was built in 1962 to link with Telstar.

THE SPACE RACE
EARLY SPACE PROBES

With the powerful rockets now available, space scientists could reach out into space, far beyond Earth, to begin exploring the other planets of the solar system. Their major targets were the Moon and the inner planets.

In 1970, Venera 7 became the first spacecraft to land on another planet and transmit data back to Earth.

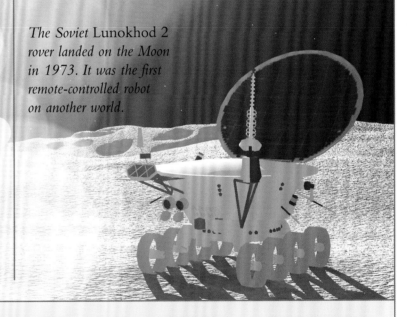

28,000 solar cells mounted on four panels provided power for Mariner 4 on its trip to Mars in 1965.

864°Fahrenheit (462°Celsius), with an atmosphere filled with deadly sulphuric acid. By 1965 the first flyby of Mars had been made, the first of many missions to the Red Planet.

The Soviet Lunokhod 2 rover landed on the Moon in 1973. It was the first remote-controlled robot on another world.

To the Moon and beyond

As the closest body to Earth in space, the Moon was an obvious target for space probes. In 1959 the Soviet probe *Luna 2* made a crash landing on the Moon's surface. A few weeks later *Luna 3* sent back the first image of the far side of the Moon, which is never visible from Earth. The first probe from Earth to reach another planet was the U.S. *Mariner 2*, which flew within 22,000 miles (35,000 km) of Venus in 1962. During the 1970s a number of Soviet Venera space probes made the first successful landings on Venus, confirming it as a hellish world,

The U.S. surveys the Moon

In 1961 President John F. Kennedy gave NASA the task of sending astronauts to the Moon. Before this could be accomplished, scientists wanted to know a lot more about this closest neighbor in space. In 1966 *Surveyor 1* became the first U.S. probe to land on the lunar surface. It showed that a soft landing on the Moon was possible—before astronauts attempted it. Four more Surveyor probes landed on the Moon before the crewed missions began.

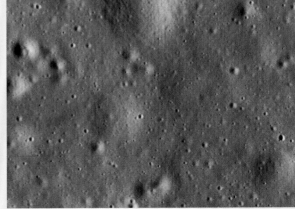

Surveyor 1 *(above) landed on the Ocean of Storms (right). It was the first U.S. space probe to soft-land on an extraterrestrial body.*

THE SPACE RACE
SPACEWALKERS

THE EARLY 1960S SAW ASTRONAUTS AND COSMONAUTS GO INTO ORBIT IN THE FIRST MULTI-CREWED SPACECRAFT. THEY ALSO SAW ASTRONAUTS AND COSMONAUTS BRAVE ENOUGH TO EXIT THEIR CAPSULES TO DRIFT IN SPACE. THE SOVIET COSMONAUT ALEXEI LEONOV BECAME THE FIRST PERSON TO WALK IN SPACE.

Voskhod

In 1964 the Soviet Union launched the first of two Voskhod spacecraft, carrying a crew of three. In March 1965 *Voskhod 2* launched with just two cosmonauts on board. The extra space was used for an inflatable airlock. Using this, Leonov exited the craft to spacewalk for just over 12 minutes. He depressurized his spacesuit on reentry in order to squeeze through the airlock's narrow entrance.

Alexei Leonov makes the first historic spacewalk from the Voskhod 2 capsule.

On June 3, 1965, Edward White became the first American to spacewalk. He used bursts of pressurized oxygen to maneuver in space.

Gemini

Project Gemini (1965–1966) was designed to test the technology needed for a trip to the Moon. The Gemini capsules carried a crew of two astronauts and were equipped with maneuvering thrusters that allowed the astronauts to change the capsule's course. This meant they could meet and dock with other spacecraft in orbit. These were skills the astronauts would need for the planned Moon missions. *Geminis VI* and *VII* met in orbit and flew within several feet, a few meters, of each other. The crews waved to each other across space. Later missions successfully docked with unmanned target vehicles that had been launched into orbit.

On January 27, 1967, during a preflight test of Apollo 1, astronauts Virgil Grissom, Edward White, and Roger Chaffee died when a fire swept through the command module.

Apollo

With the experience gained from the Gemini flights, NASA was ready to try for the Moon with Project Apollo. The Apollo spacecraft had three parts. The command module provided the crew's quarters and flight control. The service module held the propulsion and support systems. The lunar module carried two of the crew to the lunar surface and returned them to the command and service modules in lunar orbit. A number of test flights were carried out before the actual landing attempt was made. In December 1968 the *Apollo 8* astronauts became the first people to orbit the Moon.

Photographs the astronauts took of Earth gave a view of the planet that no one had seen before.

On Apollo 9 (above) the astronauts practice docking and separation of the command module and the lunar module while remaining in Earth's orbit.

THE SPACE RACE
MAN ON THE MOON

Tʜᴇ Sᴘᴀᴄᴇ Rᴀᴄᴇ ᴄᴀᴍᴇ ᴛᴏ ᴀɴ ᴇɴᴅ ɪɴ 1969, ᴡʜᴇɴ ᴛʜᴇ ᴄʀᴇᴡ ᴏғ *Aᴘᴏʟʟᴏ 11* ᴍᴀᴅᴇ Pʀᴇsɪᴅᴇɴᴛ Jᴏʜɴ F. Kᴇɴɴᴇᴅʏ's ᴅʀᴇᴀᴍ ᴏғ sᴇɴᴅɪɴɢ ᴘᴇᴏᴘʟᴇ ᴛᴏ ᴛʜᴇ Mᴏᴏɴ ᴀ ʀᴇᴀʟɪᴛʏ. Tʜᴇ ᴇᴠᴇɴᴛ ᴡᴀs ᴡᴀᴛᴄʜᴇᴅ ᴏɴ ᴛᴇʟᴇᴠɪsɪᴏɴ ʙʏ ᴍɪʟʟɪᴏɴs ᴀʀᴏᴜɴᴅ ᴛʜᴇ ᴡᴏʀʟᴅ.

Apollo 11

On July 16, 1969, *Apollo 11* astronauts Neil Armstrong, Edwin Aldrin, and Michael Collins set out on their journey to the Moon. On July 20, while Collins piloted the command module in lunar orbit, Armstrong and Aldrin took the lunar module down to the Moon's surface. After a nail-biting, boulder-dodging descent, the lunar module touched down in the Sea of Tranquility. Six hours later, Armstrong opened the hatch and stepped onto the lunar surface, the first person to set foot on a world that was not his own.

He and Aldrin spent nearly a day on the Moon, setting up experiments and collecting samples. After rejoining Collins, they returned safely to Earth on July 24.

The Saturn V *that launched the Moon missions was the most powerful rocket ever built.*

Aldrin with one of the science experiments and the Eagle *lunar module in the background*

Moon rovers

The last three Apollo missions to the Moon each carried a Lunar Roving Vehicle (LRV). The electric vehicle was designed for the low-gravity, airless conditions of the Moon. It allowed the astronauts to explore farther than they could on foot. The greatest range travelled from the lunar module was 4.7 miles (7.6 km) on the *Apollo 17* mission. The unofficial lunar land speed record of 11 miles (18 km) per hour is held by *Apollo 17*'s Eugene Cernan.

astronaut Jim Irwin with the Lunar Roving Vehicle during the Apollo 15 *mission*

THE END OF THE SPACE RACE
ERA OF THE SPACE STATIONS

With the successful conclusion of the Apollo missions, astronauts no longer travelled as far from home. Instead the USSR and the United States began to build space stations. Some were prebuilt and launched into space. Others were built in orbit around Earth.

Salyut 1, launched by the Soviet Union on April 19, 1971, was the first space station.

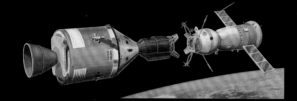

docking of Apollo with Soyuz in 1975

The first space stations

The term "space station" was invented by rocket pioneer Hermann Oberth. In 1923 he wrote of a platform orbiting Earth from which missions would leave for the Moon and Mars. The first space station was the 21-ton (19-metric ton) *Salyut 1*, launched by the USSR in 1971. The station was visited twice. The first crew failed to gain access because of a faulty hatch.

In 1973 the United States launched *Skylab*, its first space

Skylab was damaged during launch when a micrometeoroid shield separated from the workshop, tearing away one of two main solar panel arrays and jamming the other.

station. Three three-man crews occupied *Skylab* for a total of 171 days, carrying out hundreds of experiments. *Salyut* and *Skylab* were abandoned. They eventually fell back toward Earth and burned up in the atmosphere.

Handshake in space

On July 17, 1975, an Apollo spacecraft docked with a Soviet Soyuz spacecraft. The Soyuz was the Soviet Union's primary spacecraft, used since 1967 and still in service today. The Apollo-Soyuz mission tested meeting and docking systems for an international space rescue. It was the first time the two countries cooperated in space.

Working in space

Astronauts working in space face hazards unlike those found on Earth. When an astronaut leaves a capsule or space station, he or she relies on a spacesuit for protection. The suit is

In 1984 Soviet Svetlana Savitskaya became the first woman to perform a spacewalk.

equipped with oxygen, refreshments, heating and cooling equipment, and even toilet facilities. It is multilayered to protect the astronaut from micrometeoroids —tiny specks of dust flying through space at high speed. The spacesuits used today are more sophisticated than those worn by the astronauts who flew the early missions, but they have to perform the same basic functions.

astronaut Owen Garriott at work on Skylab

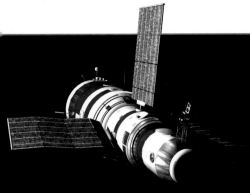

Between 1977 and 1981, Salyut 6 *was visited by 16 manned spacecraft. The longest stay onboard lasted 185 days.*

Long-duration habitation of space

Space stations gave scientists the opportunity to study the effects of spending long periods of time weightless in space. The need to know how the human body copes with this will be essential if one day astronauts set out to make the long journey to Mars and back. Astronauts who spend a long time in zero or near zero gravity can suffer a range of health problems, from dizziness to muscle wastage, and the weakening and breakdown of bones in the skeleton.

Mir

In 1986 the Soviet Union began launching the first components of the space station *Mir*. Over the course of the next decade, it was assembled in orbit and when complete was just over 60 feet (19 m) long and 100 feet (31 m) wide.

Salyut 7

It weighed nearly 285,940 pounds (129,700 kg) —over seven times more massive than *Salyut*. *Mir* supported a crew of three, with enough space to welcome an occasional guest. It orbited Earth for 15 years and was occupied for more than four-fifths of that time. Cosmonaut Valeri Polyakov flew to *Mir* on January 8, 1994, and spent the next 437 days and 18 hours aboard the space station. He returned to Earth on June 1, 1995. This set the record for the longest single human spaceflight, which still stands today. Like *Salyut* and *Skylab* before it, *Mir* fell back into the atmosphere, crashing into the South Pacific Ocean on March 23, 2001.

Mir *was the first modular space station and was assembled in orbit between 1986 and 1996.*

Living in space

Life in space is very different from life on Earth. But astronauts still need to eat, sleep, and wash. For *Mir*, menus were prepared by the cosmonauts before they left Earth and were carried to the station frozen or dehydrated. *Mir* had a shower, but it was difficult to use. The crew often resorted to wet wipes to keep clean. Exercise during long spaceflights is vital to help prevent the weakening of muscles. Simple equipment such as a treadmill onboard a space station is just as important as the science experiments.

U.S. astronaut Shannon Lucid (right) exercises on a treadmill aboard the Mir *space station.*

The Skylab 2 *crew try out the space menu during ground training (below).*

SPACE SHUTTLE
THE SPACE TRANSPORTATION SYSTEM

SPACE EXPLORATION IS A COSTLY BUSINESS. THE SPACE SHUTTLE TRANSPORTATION SYSTEM (SSTS) WAS AN ATTEMPT BY NASA TO MAKE GETTING INTO SPACE LESS EXPENSIVE BY DEVELOPING A SPACECRAFT THAT COULD BE USED AGAIN AND AGAIN. THE ONLY PART THAT WAS NOT REUSED WAS THE GIANT EXTERNAL FUEL TANK.

Launch

The shuttle orbiter was boosted into orbit by a combination of liquid fuel rockets mounted on the orbiter itself, plus a pair of solid fuel booster rockets. The boosters separated from the shuttle about two minutes after launch at a height of around 28 miles (45 km). They parachuted into the ocean and were recovered for reuse. Around 70 miles (110 km) up, the huge external fuel tank for the main engines was also jettisoned, to burn up in the atmosphere. The shuttle's main engines cut out, and its maneuvering engines fired to position the shuttle in orbit.

The shuttle was launched vertically like an ordinary rocket. The two solid rocket boosters operated in parallel with the orbiter's three main engines

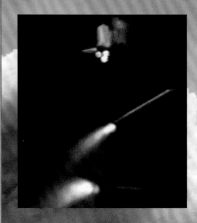

The solid rocket boosters separate from the shuttle orbiter and head to Earth to be picked up.

X-planes

The X planes (X for experimental) are a series of cutting edge aircraft built to test the limits of what can be achieved in the skies. The *X-15*, for example, was capable of flying at 50 miles (80 km) above Earth—right on the edge of space. Neil Armstrong, the first man on the Moon, was an *X-15* test pilot. The *X-24A* was used to carry out experiments in unpowered landings from high altitudes. The knowledge gained from these flights was vital in the development of the shuttle orbiter.

The X-15 (above) of the 1960s reached the edge of outer space and returned with valuable data to be used in spacecraft design. The X-24A (right) was built to test concepts that would be used in the development and design of the shuttle orbiter.

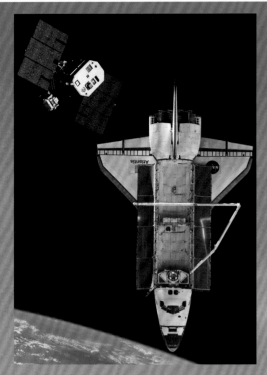

The orbiter

At take-off the shuttle orbiter weighed around 4.4 million pounds (2 million kg). It was similar in size to a small airliner and carried a crew of seven with up to 66,000 pounds (30,000 kg) of equipment. The crew's quarters were in the front of the orbiter. The upper deck of the crew compartment held the flightdeck from which the shuttle was flown. Below, on the mid deck, were the crew's living quarters. The lower deck held the life support equipment for the crew. The main part of the orbiter was the payload bay, which held the shuttle's cargo, such as satellites to be left in orbit or equipment for delivery to the *International Space Station*. Large doors opened in the payload bay to give access to the cargo.

Return to Earth

At the end of the mission, the crew would close the cargo bay doors and fire the main engines for three to four minutes, slowing the orbiter for reentry. The pilot positioned the craft to enter the atmosphere belly first so the craft was protected by its heat shield. Once back in the atmosphere, the shuttle would glide, unpowered, back to Earth—the pilot and commander curving it back and forth to adjust its speed and direction. On landing at around 220 miles (350 km) per hour, the shuttle deployed a parachute that slowed it to a halt.

The shuttle orbiter reentered the atmosphere at around 17,500 miles (28,000 km) per hour. The pilot made looping "S" turns as the orbiter glided back to the landing site.

Disasters

Astronauts accept that space travel will always be a dangerous job. In January 1986 the *Challenger* space shuttle was destroyed just 73 seconds after liftoff when a seal on a rocket booster failed. All seven crew members were killed.

In February 2003 the *Columbia* space shuttle broke up on reentering Earth's atmosphere when part of the heat shield failed. Again, all seven astronauts onboard the spacecraft died in the accident.

The space shuttle Challenger *was lost within seconds on January 28, 1986 (left).*

The space shuttle Columbia *disintegrated over Texas and Louisiana on February 1, 2003 (below).*

INTERNATIONAL SPACE STATION
(ISS)

THE *INTERNATIONAL SPACE STATION* IS A 167-FOOT (51-M), 441-TON (400-METRIC TON) PIECE OF SPACE HARDWARE. IT TOOK 10 YEARS, MORE THAN 30 MISSIONS, AND 15 COUNTRIES SHARING THEIR ENGINEERING AND SCIENTIFIC SKILLS TO PUT IT TOGETHER.

With Unity *in place, the space shuttle's robotic arm is used to join it to* Zarya.

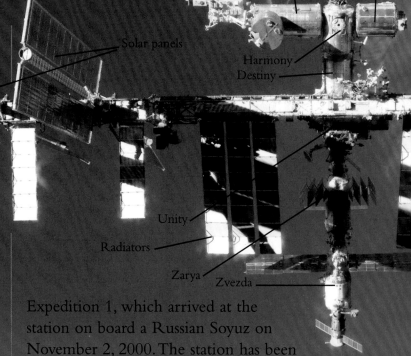

Kibo · Columbus · Solar panels · Harmony · Destiny · Unity · Radiators · Zarya · Zvezda

Building the *ISS*

The task of assembling the *ISS* began on November 20, 1998, when the first module, *Zarya*, was launched into orbit by a Russian Proton rocket. Two weeks later the NASA *Unity* module was carried up aboard the *Endeavour* space shuttle and attached to *Zarya* by spacewalking astronauts. On July 12, 2000, the *Zvezda* module was launched into orbit. Ground controllers guided the *Zarya/Unity* modules to a rendezvous and docking with *Zvezda*, using an automated system developed in Russia. *Zvezda* added sleeping quarters, exercise equipment, oxygen generators, and other equipment necessary for habitation. The *ISS* was ready for its first crew,

Expedition 1, which arrived at the station on board a Russian Soyuz on November 2, 2000. The station has been occupied since then. Over the following few years, more components were added, including laboratories, the remote-controlled robot arm, *Canadarm*, and the 230-foot (70-m) "wings" of the solar panels. In 2015 the *ISS* was being prepared to receive crewed commercial spacecraft, which could begin as soon as 2017.

Delivering the goods

As well as Soyuz and, until its retirement, the space shuttle, a number of vehicles have been used as *ISS* delivery trucks. The uncrewed Russian Progress craft is similar to Soyuz. There are between three and four Progress flights to the *ISS* each year. They carry up to 5,300 pounds (2,400 kg) of supplies on each trip. The Japanese H-II transfer vehicle carries up supplies then takes waste down to burn up in the atmosphere. Commercial spacecraft such as the SpaceX *Dragon* and Orbital ATK's *Cygnus* have also successfully flown to the *ISS*.

Soyuz spacecraft

Dragon

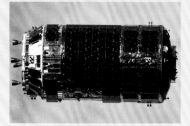

H-II Transfer Vehicle

Cygnus

Astronaut Robert Thirsk stores samples in the Minus Eighty Degree Laboratory Freezer in the Japanese Kibo laboratory aboard the ISS.

Astronaut Michael Foale conducts an experiment in the Microgravity Science Glovebox in the Destiny laboratory.

Solar panels

A giant spacelab

Staffed by six crew members, the *ISS* is a fully-equipped space research facility dedicated to the advancement of science. Thousands of experiments may be going on at any time, with many focused on the health of the astronauts who may spend several months in the low-gravity space environment. Other experiments aim to find ways to use energy more efficiently and to improve the quality of air and water. These are, of course, important concerns for the people living on the *ISS*, but it is hoped that the discoveries made there will also make life better for the rest of us on Earth.

The crew of the *ISS* can also measure changes in pollution, weather patterns, and temperature on the planet below them, providing information that will enable scientists to monitor the effects of global warming. In recent years the addition of technology such as 3-D printing, laser communications, and mini-satellite launchers has expanded the scope of what the researchers can accomplish.

The Cupola has seven windows. Added in 2010, the Cupola is the ISS's control tower. It is used to observe operations outside the station.

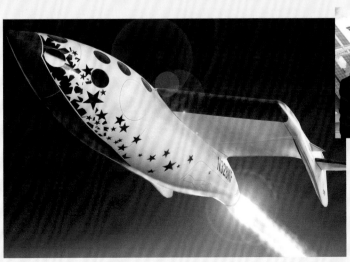

Dennis Tito (above) was the first space tourist aboard the ISS. SpaceShipOne flew 62 miles (100 km) above Earth in 2004 —the first private flight to reach space.

Space tourists

A few private individuals have been able to pay a visit to the *ISS*. Between 2001 and 2009, seven people each paid $20 million to 40 million to travel into space aboard Soyuz. The first person to do it was American multi-millionaire Dennis Tito, who spent nearly eight days aboard the *ISS* in April and May 2001.

A number of commercial companies, including SpaceX, are working on the development of craft that will be able to carry paying customers into orbit within the next few years.

EYES AND EARS IN SPACE
MODERN SATELLITES

YOU ARE BEING WATCHED. TODAY A LARGE FLEET OF SATELLITES KEEPS EARTH UNDER CONSTANT WATCH, GATHERING DATA ON A MASSIVE SCALE ABOUT OUR PLANET, ITS RESOURCES AND ITS STATE OF HEALTH. SOME TRAVEL AROUND IN LOW EARTH ORBIT. OTHERS ARE FAR OUT IN GEOSTATIONARY ORBIT.

one of six Advanced Extremely High Frequency communications satellites operated by the U.S. military

Communications satellites

Since the days of *Echo* and *Telstar*, communications satellites have come a long way. Today, a web of around 2,000 satellites orbits Earth, providing telecommunications links to all parts of the globe. A satellite link generally involves the transmission or uplinking of a signal from an Earth station to a satellite, which receives and amplifies the signal and retransmits it back to a ground station on Earth. The signals from satellites are sent on a narrow beam, so transmitting and receiving dishes are aligned with great precision.

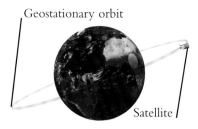

Geostationary orbit

Satellite

A geostationary orbit is one in which the satellite's orbital speed matches that of the Earth's rotation so that it seems to hang above the same point on the surface.

Earth-observing satellites

The A-train, or Afternoon constellation, are a group of six Earth-observing satellites flying one behind the other in formation around the world. They were each launched at different times between 2002 and 2014. The satellites are in a polar orbit, heading north across the equator at about 1:30 p.m. local time (hence the name of Afternoon constellation), within seconds to minutes of each other.

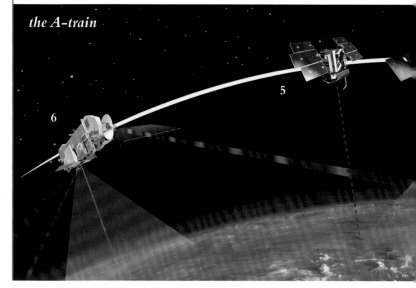

the A-train

6 5

Launching into orbit

Most satellites are sent into orbit protected inside the nose cone at the top of a rocket launcher. When orbit is achieved, the nose cone is ejected and the satellite deployed.

Depending on the mission, various types of orbit can be used. For example, an equatorial orbit circles Earth around the equator, while a polar orbit goes north to south around Earth.

A Soyuz rocket carries two Galileo satellites into space. The nose cone fairing (covering) is ejected

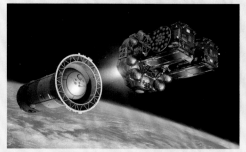

when the rocket leaves Earth's atmosphere. The upper stage then boosts the satellites up to Earth

orbit. The Galileo satellites separate and position themselves in orbit and deploy their solar panels.

They carry out a variety of observations, gathering information about Earth's atmosphere and relaying it back to scientists on the ground. The A-train is a collaboration among several countries, including the United States, Canada, Japan, and France.

1. OCO-2, launched by NASA, measures carbon dioxide levels in the atmosphere.
2. GCOM-W1, launched by Japan, observes the planet's water cycle, including sea water temperature, water levels on land, and snow depths.
3. Aqua, launched by NASA, measures temperature, water vapor in the atmosphere and rainfall.
4. CALIPSO and 5. CloudSat, launched by NASA and the French CNES, follow closely, one behind the other. Both satellites employ high-tech laser and radar instruments to build up 3-D views of clouds and airborne particles.
6. Aura, launched by NASA, studies greenhouse gases and other atmosphere features.

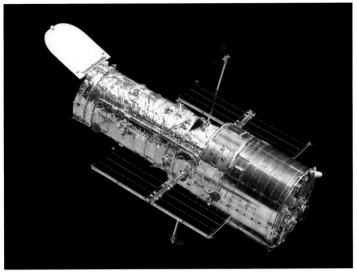

Hubble's orbit outside the distortion of Earth's atmosphere allows it to take extremely high-resolution images of distant space phenomena. It has sent back stunning images.

Space telescopes

Carried into orbit aboard the space shuttle in April 1990, the *Hubble Space Telescope* transformed our view of the universe. *Hubble* has since been joined by other space observatories, including *Chandra*, launched in July 1999, which studies x-rays from the hottest parts of the universe. The *Herschel Space Observatory* was launched in May 2009, to study the cosmos in infrared light. *Kepler*, launched in March 2009, is searching for planets around other stars. *Hubble's* successor, the *James Webb Space Telescope* is scheduled for launch in 2018.

These telescopes are all NASA projects, except for the *Herschel Space Observatory,* which was built by the European Space Agency (ESA).

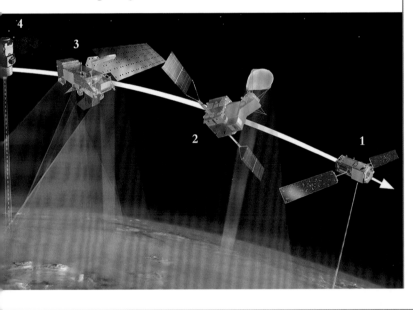

CubeSats

CubeSats, or nanosatellites, are a class of small research satellites built to a size of 4 inches (10 centimeters) each side and weighing 3 pounds (1.3 kg). Up to six of these units can be combined to make a bigger satellite. CubeSats are small enough to piggyback along with the payload of a larger mission. This means they can be added to planned launches at short notice. NASA's CubeSats are deployed using a Poly-Picosatellite Orbital Deployer, or P-POD.

CubeSats are deployed from the NanoRacks CubeSat Deployer by the Japanese robotic arm on the ISS.

MODERN SPACE PROBES
TO THE SUN, MOON, AND INNER PLANETS

THE EXPLORATION OF THE SOLAR SYSTEM IS AN ONGOING PURSUIT. CLOSEST TO HOME ARE THE ROCKY WORLDS OF MERCURY, VENUS, AND MARS, AS WELL AS THE SUN AND MOON. MARS, KNOWN AS THE "RED PLANET" BECAUSE OF THE RED RUST IN ITS SOIL, IS SIMILAR IN SIZE TO OUR PLANET, BUT IT HAS A VERY THIN ATMOSPHERE.

The Magellan *probe, which mapped the surface of Venus, was the first interplanetary mission to be launched from a space shuttle.*

Mercury and Venus

Mercury, the innermost and smallest planet of the Solar System, is difficult to study from Earth because it is never far from the glare of the Sun. So far two craft have visited Mercury, *Mariner 10* in 1974 and *MESSENGER,* which orbited Mercury from 2011 to 2015. *MESSENGER* mapped the surface of Mercury and returned valuable data about the planet, including the amazing discovery of water ice at the planet's north pole.

MESSENGER *entered orbit around Mercury on March 18, 2011, the first spacecraft to do so. It remained in orbit until 2015 when it crashed on the surface of the planet.*

Japan's *Akatsuki* space probe arrived in orbit around Venus in December 2015. Five years earlier, on its first attempt, it missed its target and had to orbit the Sun, waiting for a chance to try again. It will study the thick atmosphere of Venus. *Akatsuki* was intended to investigate Venus along with the European Space Agency's *Venus Express,* but that probe had completed its mission before *Akatsuki* arrived.

Observing the Sun

A number of missions have investigated the Sun, the star at the center of the Solar System. NASA's *Genesis* mission collected samples from the outer reaches of the Sun's atmosphere but crash landed on its return to Earth in 2004. Much of the collected material was contaminated.

The *Solar Dynamics Observatory,* launched in 2010, is part of NASA's "Living With a Star" program, which aims to understand how changes in the Sun can affect life on Earth.

Genesis *collected a sample of solar wind and returned it to Earth for analysis.*

Mars

More probes have visited Mars than have been sent to any one of the other planets. But becauseof the difficulties of space exploration, around two-thirds of them have failed before they could carry out their missions. Currently four orbiters and four landers are sending back streams of data about Mars. *MAVEN*, a NASA orbiter, arrived in September 2014. It aims to answer important questions about the climate on Mars and the forces at work in the Martian atmosphere. The *Mars Reconnaissance Orbiter* has been returning data since 2006, using the most powerful camera yet sent to Mars to search for evidence of past water and to map out landing sites for future Mars missions.

The car-sized robotic rover Curiosity *is currently exploring Gale Crater on Mars as part of NASA's Mars Science Laboratory mission.*

The Mars Exploration Rover *Opportunity* has been travelling the Martian surface since 2004. It has covered more than 18 miles (30 km) from its landing site and has recently been investigating a crater. *Curiosity*, which arrived in August 2012, is a "next generation" rover. It landed in Gale Crater and found material deposited by a long vanished lake. The rover has made some key discoveries, such as the detection of organic material.

Asteroids and comets

Space missions to some of the Solar System's smaller objects have been among the most exciting and successful of recent years. In 2014 the European Space Agency's Rosetta *went into orbit around a comet (67P) and sent a probe down onto its surface. NASA's* Dawn *probe arrived at the asteroid Ceres in 2015 and entered orbit around the minor planet, sending back stunning images.*

The Philae lander approaches comet 67P.

Moon probes

Dozens of probes have studied the Moon, and it is the only world other than our own that humans have visited. The Chinese *Chang'e 3* orbiter and rover arrived in December 2013.

Also Chinese, the *Yutu* (Jade Rabbit) rover landed and sent back images of the lunar surface, but a system failure left it unable to move and explore.

NASA's *Lunar Reconnaissance* orbiter has been sending high resolution images of the entire lunar surface back to Earth since it entered orbit in 2009.

During its seven-month mission the Lunar Atmosphere and Dust Environment Explorer (LADEE) *used its instruments to study dust and gases in the lunar exosphere from orbit. The mission ended on April 18, 2014, when the spacecraft's controllers intentionally crashed the probe on the lunar far side.*

MODERN SPACE PROBES
TO THE OUTER PLANETS AND BEYOND

SPACESHIPS FROM EARTH HAVE VISITED ALL OF THE PLANETS IN THE SOLAR SYSTEM, INCLUDING THOSE MOST DISTANT FROM THE SUN. TWO OF THESE ROBOT EXPLORERS HAVE EVEN GONE FARTHER AND ARE NOW SENDING BACK INFORMATION FROM BEYOND THE SOLAR SYSTEM.

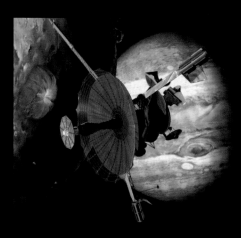

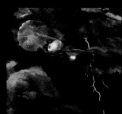

Galileo's probe (above) descends into Jupiter's atmosphere. Galileo passes Io with Jupiter in the background (left).

Galileo and *Juno*

NASA's *Galileo* mission to Jupiter and its moons, which ended in 2003, was a huge success. In 1993, on its way to the giant planet, it became the first probe to fly by an asteroid, and in 1994 it saw the comet Shoemaker–Levi 9 crash into Jupiter. Once *Galileo* reached Jupiter, it discovered evidence of the existence of a saltwater ocean beneath the icy surface of Jupiter's moon Europa, which scientists think

may hold life. It also detected volcanic activity on the moon Io, 100 times greater than that on Earth. *Galileo* plunged into Jupiter's atmosphere on September 21, 2003, to avoid hitting Europa.

The *Juno* spacecraft arrived in Jupiter's orbit in 2016 with plans to study the composition of the planet and try to discover how it formed. It is powered by the largest solar panels ever used on an interplanetary probe.

Juno, launched by NASA, entered Jupiter's orbit on July 4, 2016.

Beyond the Solar System

Since August 2012 NASA scientists have been in constant contact with a spacecraft in interstellar space—the space between stars. This craft is *Voyager 1*, the farthest travelled of all our probes, which passed through the boundary of the heliosphere—the region of space dominated by the Sun. The twin *Voyager 1* and *2*

spacecraft set out on their journey in 1977. Their main mission was to explore Jupiter and Saturn. *Voyager 2* went on to Uranus and Neptune.

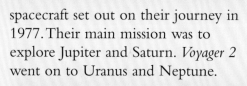

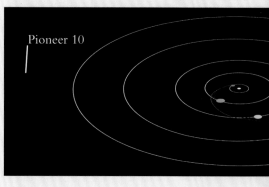

Pioneer 10

Pioneer 11 left Earth in 1973. It is one of four manmade probes now leaving the Solar System. Contact was lost in 1995, but it is thought to be 8.7 billion miles (14 billion km) out from the Sun.

Cassini-Huygens

The amazingly successful *Cassini-Huygens* mission to the ringed planet Saturn was a joint enterprise between NASA and the European Space Agency. *Cassini*, which reached Saturn in 2004, is one of the most sophisticated of the deep space explorers. It carried a probe called *Huygens*, which parachuted to the surface of Saturn's largest moon, Titan, in January 2005. It sent back a stream of information about a moon that is actually bigger than the planet Mercury. In late 2016 *Cassini* will make a daring set of orbits called the Grand Finale. After a final flyby of Titan, *Cassini* will swoop between Saturn's upper atmosphere and its innermost ring, collecting information about the planet and the rings.

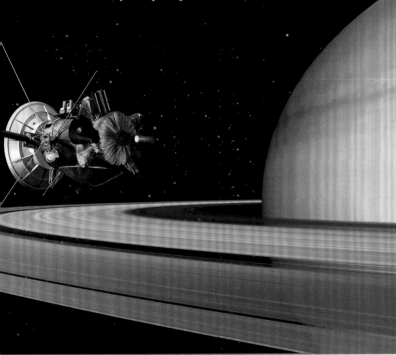

Cassini *was the first space probe to orbit around Saturn.*

In 2015 New Horizons *flew within 7,800 miles (12,500 km) of Pluto, the first spacecraft to reach it.*

New Horizons

When the *New Horizons* probe reached the dwarf planet Pluto, it sent back breathtaking images of a world on the outer reaches of the Solar System. Even the *Hubble Space Telescope* only showed it as a fuzzy blob. Pluto is part of the Kuiper Belt, a region of strange objects left over from the formation of the Solar System that scientists want to explore.

It is still the only spacecraft to have visited the giant planets. *Voyager 2* is currently travelling through the heliosheath, the outermost layer of the heliosphere, and will reach interstellar space in 2017. Both spacecraft still send back information through the Deep Space Network. The Voyager spacecraft have enough power and fuel to function until at least 2020. By then, *Voyager 1* will be 13.8 billion miles (22.1 billion km) and *Voyager 2* 11.4 billion miles (18.4 billion km) from the Sun.

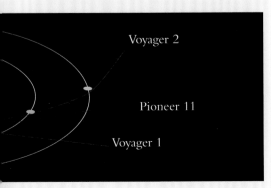

Voyager 2

Pioneer 11

Voyager 1

On August 25, 2012, data from Voyager 1 *indicated that it had become the first manmade object to leave the Solar System and enter interstellar space, where no one has gone before.*

SPACE EXPLORATION
THE FUTURE

THE POSSIBILITIES FOR THE FUTURE OF SPACE EXPLORATION MAY BE AS LIMITLESS AS SPACE ITSELF. NEW PROPULSION SYSTEMS WILL ALLOW MUCH MORE EFFICIENT MISSIONS. PEOPLE MAY SOON RETURN TO THE MOON AND PERHAPS TRAVEL ON TO MARS. AND ONE DAY, WHO KNOWS, PEOPLE MIGHT EVEN REACH THE STARS.

Rocket systems

The Space Launch System (SLS), currently being developed as NASA's new launch vehicle, will be the most powerful rocket ever built by NASA. It will launch crews of up to four astronauts in the *Orion* spacecraft as well as sending robot probes to destinations such as Mars, Jupiter, and Saturn. The first SLS rocket is due at NASA's Kennedy Space Center in Florida in 2018. NASA is also working on a Solar Electric Propulsion (SEP) project that will generate electric power from solar panels, to fire high energy gas from the thruster. The SEP will use 10 times less propellant than other systems.

NASA's Space Launch System will be the powerhouse of its space exploration, launching probes across the Solar System and possibly sending the first people to Mars.

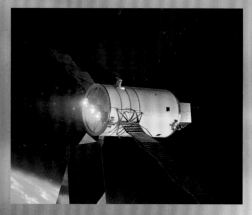

SEP could be the way forward for exploration in deep space.

Near future

There is much to look forward to in space exloration. The scheduled launch of the *James Webb Space Telescope* will open up a new window on the universe.

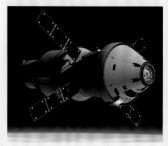

The Orion Multi-Purpose Crew Vehicle is intended to carry a crew of four astronauts on missions to Earth orbit —and beyond.

Japan's *Hayabusa 2* space probe is on its way to asteroid 162173 Ryugu and is expected to arrive there in July 2018. It will survey the asteroid for a year and a half before heading back to Earth in December 2019 with a sample of the asteroid. The return journey will take a year.

New Horizons continues its journey through the Kuiper Belt and will fly past another object in 2019.

The first crewed flight of the new *Orion* spacecraft is scheduled for 2023.

The James Webb Space Telescope *is being developed by NASA and the European Space Agency and is scheduled to launch in 2018.*

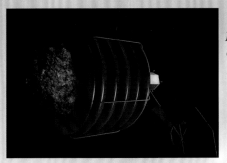

One day it may be possible to capture asteroids and mine them for their resources.

Asteroids and the Moon

NASA is planning a mission to collect a multi-ton boulder from the surface of an asteroid and redirect it into an orbit around the Moon. Astronauts aboard NASA's *Orion* spacecraft, to be launched from an SLS rocket, will visit the asteroid boulder in the mid-2020s. They will return with samples to be studied on Earth.

The Asteroid Redirect Mission (ARM) will be a test of the technologies and spaceflight skills that will be needed ahead of a human mission to Mars. The asteroid boulder will be moved using the SEP system. NASA plans to launch the ARM robotic spacecraft in 2019.

Russia, China, India, Japan, and the European Space Agency have all declared their intentions to continue the exploration of the Moon, including establishing moonbases. Japan and India hope to have achieved this goal by 2030.

a futuristic view of a base on Mars

Mission to Mars

Robot explorers have been visiting Mars for more than 40 years. People may join them by the 2030s. Astronauts aboard the *International Space Station* have learned a lot about body changes over long periods in space. Even a short Mars trip would mean 400 to 450 days in space. The Mars mission will be built around the *Orion* spacecraft and the Space Launch System. The commercial company SpaceX plans a Mars Colonial Transporter program, sending people to Mars in 2024 and returning them to Earth. After that the colonization of Mars can begin.

How a future Moon base might look.

Interstellar space exploration

People cannot travel to the stars yet. The distances involved are immense. To reach the nearest star in less than 100 years, a ship would have to reach a speed of 30 million miles (50 million km) per hour. A reliable engine using nuclear fuel will be needed to make it possible. For now we have to do our interstellar exploration from afar, by means of space observatories such as the *Hubble Space Telescope* and, from 2018, the *James Webb Space Telescope*.

A propulsion system that can accelerate a ship to colossal speeds is needed in order to reach the stars.

GLOSSARY

airlock
An airtight room with two entrances that allows an astronaut to secure the air in the spacecraft behind one door before opening the other door to exit the spacecraft.

antenna
A device that detects and transmits signals such as radio waves.

asteroid
Sometimes called minor planets, these are rocky objects orbiting the Sun in the Solar System, mostly between the orbits of Mars and Jupiter. They vary greatly in size from hundreds of miles to just a few miles across.

astronaut
A person who is trained to travel in space.

atmosphere
The layer of gases and dust particles that surround a planet.

ballistic missile
A missile that travels a long distance on a high arching flightpath. It is boosted up from the ground by a rocket engine then falls back to Earth under the pull of gravity.

bogie
A separate four- or six-wheeled undercarriage positioned beneth a heavy vehicle to help it move.

booster
The first, most powerful, stage of a rocket that lifts it off the ground.

comet
A fairly small (just a few miles across) object that orbits the Sun. Comets are mostly made of ice and dust and produce a long tail of dust and gas when their orbit brings them close to the Sun.

cosmonaut
A Russian astronaut.

engineer
A person who designs or builds engines, machines or buildings.

equator
The line around Earth midway between the north and south poles.

extraterrestrial
Something that is not from Earth.

geostationary orbit
An orbit in which the satellite matches the speed of rotation of Earth so that it appears to keep station above the same point on the surface. This happens when the orbit is 22,300 miles (35,900 km) above the equator.

global warming
The gradual increase in the temperature of Earth's atmosphere, which most scientists believe is caused by human activities. Global warming is likely to result in climate change.

gravity
The force of attraction between objects, which is particularly great for massive objects, such as planets and stars.

gyro
Short for gyroscope, a device that is used to provide stability.

heliosheath
The zone that marks the outer border of the Solar System where the heliosphere gives way to interstellar space.

heliosphere
The region of space that is dominated by the influence of the Sun.

interstellar space
The space between the stars.

micrometeoroid
A dust-sized particle in space. Despite its small size, its high velocity means it can cause significant damage to spacecraft and satellites.

moon
Space object that orbits a planet. Earth has one moon that is usually known as the Moon. Other planets have moons too.

nanosatellite
A satellite that weighs between 2.2 and 22 pounds (1 and 10 kg), including fuel.

orbit
The path an object in space follows around a larger object, such as Earth's path around the Sun or a satellite's path around Earth.

organic
Something that is related to, or which comes from, living things.

planet
Large space object that is spherical in shape and follows a regular path in orbit around a star.

propulsion
The force that moves something forward.

radiation
Energy in the form of electromagnetic waves (x-rays, light, infrared, and radio waves, for example) or as high energy atomic particles.

range
The distance a vehicle can travel, often determined by the amount of its fuel supply.

reentry
The return of a spacecraft into the atmosphere surrounding Earth.

satellite
An artificial space probe placed in orbit around Earth or another object in space to gather information. Also a natural object orbiting a larger one. The Moon is a satellite of Earth.

solar panel
A device that converts light energy into electrical energy.

sounding rocket
Also called a research rocket—one that carries scientific instruments into the upper atmosphere for study but does not enter orbit.

Soviet Union
Union of Soviet Socialist Republics—a former federation of communist republics, created from the Russian Empire after the 1917 Russian Revolution.

star
Space object that becomes large and dense enough to undergo fusion and give out light and heat. Earth's Sun is a star.

suborbital
The path followed by a sounding rocket, taking it to the edge of space but not into orbit.

INDEX

A-train, 22-23
Akatsuki, 24
Aldrin, Edwin, 15
Apollo, 14, 15, 16
Armstrong, Neil, 15, 18
Asteroid Redirect
    Mission, 29
Atlas D rocket, 11

Bell X-1, 8

Cape Canaveral, 8, 9
Cassini-Huygens, 27
Chaffee, Roger, 14
Challenger, 19
*Chandra Space
    Observatory*, 23
Chang'e 3, 25
Collins, Michael, 15
Columbia, 19
communications
    satellites, 12, 22
Congreve, Sir William, 4
CubeSats, 23
Curiosity rover, 25

Dawn, 25

Echo 1, 12
European Space Agency,
    4, 24, 25, 29
Expedition 1, 20
Explorer, 9, 12

Gagarin, Yuri, 10
Galileo, 22, 26
Genesis, 24
Glenn, John, 11
Goddard, Robert, 6, 9
Grissom, Virgil, 14

Ham (chimpanzee), 11

Hayabusa 2, 28
*Herschel Space
    Observatory*, 23
Hubble Space Telescope, 19,
    23

Intercontinental ballistic
    missile (ICBM), 8
*International Space
    Station* (ISS), 4, 19,
    20-21

*James Webb Space
    Telescope*, 23, 28
Jodrell Bank
    Observatory, 12
Juno, 26
Jupiter, 26

*Kepler Space
    Observatory*, 23
Korolev, Sergei, 7, 8, 10
Kuiper Belt, 27, 28

Laika, 9, 10
Leonov, Alexei, 14
Lippisch, Alexander, 7
Luna, 13
*Lunar Atmosphere and
    Dust Environment
    Explorer*, 25
Lunar Roving Vehicle, 15

Magellan, 24
Mariner, 13
Mars, 25, 29
*Mars Colonial
    Transporter*, 29
*Mars Reconnaissance
    Orbiter*, 25
MAVEN, 25
Mercury, 24

Mercury capsule, 11
MESSENGER, 24
Messerschmitt Me 163
    Komet, 7
Mir, 17
Moon, 13, 14, 15, 25, 29

National Aeronautics and
    Space Administration
    (NASA), 9, 13, 24, 25,
    28, 29
New Horizons, 27, 28

Oberth, Hermann, 6, 7,
    9, 16
Opportunity rover, 25
Orbital ATK *Cygnus*, 20
Orion spacecraft, 28

Pioneer 11, 26
Pluto, 27
Polyakov, Valeri, 17
Progress, 20
Project Apollo, 14, 15
Project Gemini, 14
Project Mercury, 11

R-7 rocket, 8, 9, 10, 11
Redstone rocket, 8, 11
Rosetta, 25
RTV G-4 Bumper
    rocket, 9
Ruggieri, Claude, 4

Salyut 1, 16
Sander, Wilhelm
    Freidrich, 6
Saturn, 27
Saturn V rocket, 15
Shepard, Alan, 11
Skylab, 16

*Solar Dynamics
    Observatory*, 24
Solar Electric
    Propulsion, 28
Soyuz 1, 6, 20, 22
Space Launch System, 28
space shuttle, 18-19, 23
space stations, 16, 17
SpaceShipOne, 21
Space Shuttle
    Transportation System
    (SSTS), 18–19
space telescopes, 23
space tourists, 21
SpaceX, 20, 21, 29
Sputnik, 8, 9, 12
Surveyor 1, 13
Syncom 3, 12

Telstar, 12
Tereshkova, Valentina, 10
TIROS 1, 12
Tito, Dennis, 21
Tsiolkovsky, Konstantin,
    6, 9

V-2 rocket, 7, 8
Valie, Max, 6
Vanguard, 8, 12
Venera 7, 13
Venus, 13, 24
Von Braun, Wernher, 7, 8
Voskhod 2, 14
Vostok, 10, 11
Voyager, 26, 27

White, Edward, 14

X-planes, 18

Yeager, Charles, 8